Sports World

Tennis

Donna Bailey

I am going to learn to play tennis.
My tennis coach told Dad which
tennis racket to buy for me.
My racket is light with a short handle.

I must get the right shoes to wear.
Tennis shoes have special soles.
They stop you from slipping on
the tennis court.

First, we bounce the ball up and down
on our tennis rackets.
This helps us learn to control the ball.

4

Our tennis coach shows me how
to hold my racket.
This is the way to hold it for
a forehand stroke.

We practice swinging our rackets
backward and forward.
This will help our forehand stroke.

6

Our coach then shows me how to change
my grip for a backhand stroke.
I hold the racket with my other hand
to change my grip.

This is the way to hold the racket
for a backhand stroke.

Our coach shows us how to swing
the racket to hit the ball in
a backhand stroke.

Now we practice the swing for
the backhand stroke.

On the court, our coach tells us
to stand sideways to the net.
We try to lean slightly forward.

My partner sends the ball over
the net to me.
I wait until the ball bounces to strike it.
I return the ball with a forehand swing.

Now our coach shows us how to serve.
Before the serve, I hold the ball
against the racket.

Then I throw the ball up in the air.
I keep my eyes on the ball as
I swing my racket back.

I try to hit the ball at its
highest point.

15

Now we play a game together.
My partner serves and I try
to hit the ball back to her.

16

As I get better, I learn to move
around the court.
I watch the ball all the time.
I always try to be in the right place
to hit the ball when it bounces.

A tennis court has white markings for
singles and for doubles games.
The area for a doubles game is wider
because there are four players.

It is important to check the height of
the net before the game begins.

The game begins with a serve.
The server tries to hit the ball over the net.
If the ball does not go over the net after
two tries, the other player gets a point.

The server serves from the base line
at the back of the court.
The server has to hit the ball into
the opposite quarter just across the net.
This quarter is called the service court.

When the ball bounces in the service court,
the other player moves forward.
The player hits the ball back and
the rally begins.

If the other player misses the ball,
or hits it out of the court,
he loses the point.

The umpire calls a fault if a player
hits the ball out of bounds.
The other player then gets the point.
The score is shown on a large board.

Partners in a doubles match
must work together.
Each player is responsible
for one part of the court.

Many important tennis tournaments
are held each year.
The main team competition for men
is the Davis Cup.

This is Zina Garrison.

She is competing for the Wightman Cup.

It is a team competition for women.

Wimbledon is played on a grass court.
In 1985, Boris Becker was the youngest man
to become a Wimbledon champion.
He was only 17 years old.

The United States Open Championships
are played at Flushing Meadow
in New York City.

The first tennis games were played in Europe.
Now tennis is played in nearly
every country of the world.

Young players can learn short tennis.
Short tennis is played on a smaller court
than regular tennis.
In short tennis, players use plastic rackets
and a foam ball.

Even young players sometimes
compete in tournaments.
Tennis is a game people
of all ages enjoy.

Index

Editorial Consultant: Donna Bailey
Executive Editor: Elizabeth Strauss
Project Editor: Becky Ward

Picture research by Jennifer Garratt
Designed by Richard Garratt Design

Photographs
All photographs by Peter Greenland except:
Agence Vandystadt: 26 (Christophe Guibbaud)
All Sport: 27 (Bob Martin); 29 (Mike Powell)

Library of Congress Cataloging-in-Publication Data: Bailey, Donna. Tennis / Donna Bailey. p. cm.—
(Sports world) Includes index. Summary: Beginners learn the skills, techniques, and rules of tennis.
ISBN 0-8114-2904-0 1. Tennis—Juvenile literature. [1. Tennis.] I. Title. II. Series: Bailey, Donna.
Sports world. GV996.5.B33 1991 796.342—dc20 90-23056 CIP AC

ISBN 0-8114-2904-0

1 2 3 4 5 6 7 8 9 0 LB 96 95 94 93 92 91

DATE DUE
